Isaac William Wiley

Two Lectures on the Rebellion

How We Got In, How to Get Out

Isaac William Wiley

Two Lectures on the Rebellion
How We Got In, How to Get Out

ISBN/EAN: 9783743389830

Manufactured in Europe, USA, Canada, Australia, Japa

Cover: Foto ©Suzi / pixelio.de

Manufactured and distributed by brebook publishing software
(www.brebook.com)

Isaac William Wiley

Two Lectures on the Rebellion

TWO LECTURES

ON

THE REBELLION.

SUBJECTS:

HOW WE GOT IN.

HOW TO GET OUT.

DELIVERED AT

TEMPERANCE HALL, TRENTON, N. J.,

By Rev. I. W. WILEY, A. M., M. D.

REPORTED BY JAMES RISTINE, A. M.,

For the Benefit of the Sanitary Commission.

SECOND EDITION.

TRENTON, N. J.

THOMAS U. BAKER, PRINTER.

1864.

ON

THE REBELLION.

SUBJECTS:

HOW WE GOT IN.
HOW TO GET OUT.

DELIVERED AT

TEMPERANCE HALL, TRENTON, N. J.,

By Rev. I. W. WILEY, A. M., M. D.

REPORTED BY JAMES RISTINE, A. M.,

For the Benefit of the Sanitary Commission.

SECOND EDITION.

TRENTON, N. J.
THOMAS U. BAKER, PRINTER.
1864.

PREFACE.

The following Lectures were delivered at the request of many citizens of Trenton, in behalf of the Sanitary Commission. The subjects of the Lectures were also assigned me, almost in the words which I have used in their titles. Ill health prevented me from any extended preparation for them, and they were delivered extemporaneously, being taken down by Mr. Ristine, with great accuracy, as they were spoken. In this form they appear; I have made but few changes in the reported copy, preferring that they should go forth as the free and spontaneous utterance of the occasion. As such, of course, they lay no claim to any literary merit, nor do I hold myself responsible for their publication, this being the work of the Committee. If their delivery in Temperance Hall, or their subsequent publication and circulation, shall in any way contribute to a better understanding of our present struggle, and to a more earnest loyalty to our noble government, I shall be abundantly compensated for all part I have had in the work.

I. W. WILEY.

Trenton, March 1, 1864.

HOW WE GOT IN.

Ladies and Gentlemen, Fellow Citizens:

I am glad to be able to meet you on this occasion, after having been under the necessity of disappointing you some weeks ago. I have much recovered my health, but still am laboring under some difficulties, and shall speak to-night somewhat under embarrassment on account of that illness.

There are speakers whom we have heard, who always have to say something before they begin; and it seems to me altogether right and necessary that I should say something of my personal character, before entering directly upon the subject of my lecture.

I have been invited by some citizens of Trenton to deliver these two lectures, or otherwise I would much rather have remained at home, and kept still; but being called upon for this service, I am ready to render this, as all other services in my power, to promote the welfare of our country; to lead to a better understanding of the difficulties we are in; to point, if possible, to the way to get out, and in any way to contribute to the establishment and perpetuity of our great and good government. And yet there are men known to many of you, belonging to different classes, and holding different positions in life from that occupied by me, that doubtless would treat these questions in a much more able manner than I shall be able to do. I am not a politician, and still less a partizan; therefore, I do not recognize this invitation as coming from politicians, or from any partizans, and I do not feel to-night that I am here to plead the cause of any party, or to speak in behalf of any particular view of the question which shall come before us. I am not a statesman. I have never enjoyed any of the public or official positions of the country, and I am very sure I have no wish to enjoy any of these positions. I stand before you in the character simply of an American citizen, one that loves my country, who loves to study its history, and with an honest heart, desires to find out what are the difficulties that are now hanging over this nation. It has been my duty in one position I have occupied, to be a student of history, and I have had some experience in this matter. My duty has called me to study the history of our own country, and when I take up a question of the kind, I shall discuss it simply in a historical manner ; tracing out the causes that have led to the present Rebellion, by a review of the history of our country ; and as I have no partizan objects to gain, and no party to please, none to commend and none to condemn, it shall be my simple business, as far as I possibly can, and with as little prejudice as possible, to review these circumstances, and to bring out from our history the facts that bear directly upon these results that are now before us.   I must be permitted further to say, that if I should bring out here to night some facts that may strike you as novel, you must still allow me the honesty of simply presenting them as facts, in my view.   If I should state some things contrary to your prejudices, still you must not look upon me as the author of the facts, or simply announcing them, as constituting either approval or disapproval of the facts themselves.   With these preliminary observations I start the question, How came we in the present war ?   What were the causes operating in the past, that have brought into our country this great Rebellion ?   And I answer three; if I should have time I would introduce a fourth.   I think we will have time to discuss only three.

' The first is this : THE WANT OF HOMOGENEOUSNESS IN THE POPULATIONS OF OUR COUNTRY ; the second, THE GROWING POLITICAL CORRUPTION IN THE ADMINISTRATION OF OUR GOVERNMENT ; the third, ACTUAL COLLISIONS WITH THE GOVERNMENT OF OUR COUNTRY, *the last of which constitutes the Rebellion itself.*

I say then the first cause that led to this Rebellion is, *a want of unity or homogeneousness in the population of the country itself.*   Now when we come to consider a great question like this, What has brought on this gigantic war ? of course we cannot trace it to causes immediately preceding the outbreaking of the Rebellion ; to mere superficial circumstances of momentary operation among the people ; but it must be traced back to deeper principles, lying in the constitution of the country itself. There are deeper causes than those that float upon the surface ; and among those deeper influences that have led to this Rebellion is the one that I have mentioned—*we have not been one people.*   By it I mean simply this—that while throughout our nation we have many things in common, and there are many national characteristics in which we agree, there are many things in which we disagree, and have disagreed from the commencement of our history.   It requires but a little study of our history and little observation of our national life, to find that we have in this country at least two people, and have had from the origin of the country itself; and that the distinctions between these two people have been showing themselves in all our past history, and are now exhibited most prominently in the Rebellion that is upon the land. If for instance we go back to glance at the origin of our country, at its settlement by our fathers, we see that two classes of people came to this country, and originally settled the colonies. We remember that one class who came as our fathers, came driven out from their homes under the operation of great religious and national influences, and came to this country under these impulses, inspired with noble motives, sighing after liberty, seeking for a quiet place in which they might worship God, entering into covenant relations with the Most High as they were on the ocean voyage, and committing themselves and all their descendants to a perpetuation of this covenant in all coming time. We know also in another part of our country, many of the colonies were settled on the mere principle of wild adventure, of large and unscrupulous speculation, of extravagant anticipations of wealth, a heroic rushing out to find vast territories and to accumulate vast treasures. Permit me here to make this preliminary remark; when I say we have two people in this country, I mean we have one people in the North and one people in the South, I mean the dividing line that separates these two classes is the line sometimes called Mason and Dixon's line, and I wish the remarks I have made to apply in this respect. I would qualify it simply with regard to Virginia, Delaware and Maryland, lying upon the south side of this line. With regard to these states we have some exceptions in their settlement and historical development; and as we look at the history of these states, at their sympathy and co-operation in the battle of the Revolution, and the maintenance of our government, we can see there was a difference in the origin and settlement and spirit of these states. But passing farther south, the remarks I made apply strictly to the Carolinas, to Georgia and Alabama, and still more strictly to that large territory occupied at the commencement of our government, and at the time of our Revolution, by an entirely different people from us, I mean of course Florida, and the large territory known originally under the name of Louisiana, occupied by Frenchmen, by Spaniards, and by half-breeds, since purchased by our government, and having still large numbers of their descendants occupying these states. I say then, in our historical origin, in the settlement of our country, we see that the people of the two sides of this line have started out with different principles and moved under different impulses; the one sighing for a civilization higher than they had yet reached at home, panting for religious liberty, for a free and enlightened commonwealth; the other launching out simply with an adventurous spirit to settle a nation and found an empire, with but little reference as to what should be its characteristics or spirit. Now go a little farther forward in our history to the time of our Revolution, and you will find in this great struggle to gain the liberty of our country, again we stood forth as two people, excepting to some considerable extent the three states that I have mentioned. When the tocsin of war was sounded for the great battle of freedom, the North rallied to a man. New England poured out her fathers and sons : Virginia stood side by side with New England, and Maryland and Delaware did the same. The Carolinas hesitated, South Carolina stood coolly back, and threw the weight of her influence on the side of Great Britain. When we go back to trace the history of those " times that tried men's souls" we find, true as history itself, that within the borders of little South Carolina, there were more tories and traitors to the contest for liberty, than in all the other states put together. Here they gathered, until the government, oppressed by the schemes and plottings of these Carolinians, sent down that grand old hero, General Marion, who, by his conduct there, won for himself the title of the " American Fox," to hunt them out in South Carolina, and destroy the influence and power of those traitors who were working for the enemy. (Applause.) Does this seem like a severe charge against a sister state? Let us refer to a fact or two in the history of the times. In the spring of 1780, Sir Henry Clinton and Vice Admiral Arbuthnot, in command of the British naval forces, presented themselves in Charleston harbor, and actually demanded the surrender of that city. General Lincoln as boldly defied the challenge of these British officers, and said "if they wanted any American soil it was their duty to come and take it." Lincoln was a good name you see in 1780. (Applause.) The South Carolinians have hated the name ever since. (Laughter and applause.) Immediately after this truly American and patriotic reply had been given by General Lincoln, two hundred and twenty-six citizens of that city (Charleston) signed a letter written to Sir Henry Clinton, a most beggarly entreatment that he should reject the reply of Lincoln as in no way representing the spirit of South Carolina, that yet owed its allegiance to his majesty of England—the most pusillanimous letter that was ever written in all the history of our Revolution. At the same time they charged upon the Northern States the guilt of the Revolution and declared to Sir Henry Clinton, that the inhabitants of South Carolina, and including—not perhaps unauthorizedly—Georgia, had no sympathy with this, as they styled it, " rank democracy," which the men of the North wished to establish; on the contrary they desired nothing better than obedience to his majesty, George of England, and pledged themselves to use all exertions in the furtherance of the designs of Sir

Henry Clinton. Clinton wrote immediately to the Secretary of State of Great Britain this fact, and concluded his letter by saying, "I may truly say that within the state of South Carolina we have either every man upon our side, or the few that are against us are prisoners in our hands." You see then we have but to appeal to the history of the past to find that at the commencement, these people entered into no sympathy with the Republican institutions of our country. Let me call your attention especially to the remark in the letter of these men denouncing the "rank democracy of the North." That is it. From the commencement they have been in no sympathy with the Republican and Democratic institutions of our land. They are men who love monarchy, who sigh for it, and who wish to be recognized in our whole land as the chivalry of the nation, ready not only to throw off the yoke of the government under which they have lived, but in a spirit similar to that of the past, to secure for themselves a monarchy again.

Let us look a little farther. When we came to enter the original compact for fighting the battle of freedom, again we find the North, including the three Southern states I have named, heartily entering into that compact, and esteeming even the articles of confederation as a sacred and perpetual obligation ; that for the present they were to minister to the great work of guiding the country through the Revolution, and then were to be developed into a more permanent and binding compact for the nation. South Carolina and Georgia refused at first to enter. It was not until two years of Revolutionary struggle had passed that these two states accepted the articles of Confederation, and they never came into the compact with any other interpretation, than that it was a mere temporary arrangement for fighting the battle of the Revolution, and which, when the war was over, was to leave these states sovereign in themselves as before. And when, in 1788, the new constitution was presented to the new nation—the old articles of Confederation having been found insufficient—again we find these two states holding back most strenuously against accepting the new constitution, and for the very same reasons that they have been urging in our ears ever since, and which have culminated in the Rebellion. What reasons?

First. *We are independent and sovereign states, and refuse to yield our independence and sovereignty to a bond like this.*

Second. *We look at the articles of your constitution, and find in it no guarantee* (to use the language of the times that we have grown familiar with), *nothing to secure and guarantee to us the peculiar institution that characterizes the South.*

Not until that Constitution was so modified as to allow them tacitly to interpret it as a temporary compact, and to introduce a guarantee both for slavery and the slave trader, did this proud little Miss Carolina of the South consent to associate with her sister states in this Union. Now then a step farther.

What man who has travelled in our country and crossed the line that divides the North and South, has not felt that in passing from the North into that South, he has entered a new atmosphere; he gets among a new people. The form of life, the customs of society, the institutions of the people, the spirit, the whole tone of civilization of the Southern country, strikes him at once as different from that in which he lived in the North. The Southern gentleman is different from the Northern gentleman. The Northern gentleman is a man of industry, a man who honors labor, that is not ashamed to toil for his own good and for the good of his fellows, and he may come from his workshop, from behind his counter, out of his office, away from his business, whatever it may be, and feel that he is one of "nature's noblemen," clothed in a different garb of civilized and social life. He feels he is a man because he is a laborer, a laborer for God—a laborer for his fellow man.

The Southern gentleman is a man who is dressed in broadcloth, with an exceedingly large watch-chain dangling in front, a considerable amount of hirsuteness in his face, and an immeasurable amount of self-conceit and bold defiance in his demeanor. Go to any of our watering places, and without a microscope or telescope you can point out without difficulty who is the Northern and who is the Southern gentleman. You can see one staid, upright, thoughtful, honest, honorable, and the other gene- rally—of course I admit many honorable exceptions—a swaggerer, a boaster, a smoker, a chewer, and a man who puts himself outside of a glass of brandy as quickly as any gustatory experiment you ever saw. (Laughter.)

In the North again, progress is the spirit of our national life, and as a foundation for a free Republican commonwealth, we have struggled to elevate the masses. We have built the free church; we have established the free pulpit; we have instituted the free school; we have insisted upon the free press; and we have been proud when we have been able to establish institutions that would elevate the humble and poor, and lift them to higher levels of life. Now pass this line and all is changed. You must not have a free pulpit; why? The preacher might say some- thing about *something*. (Laughter.) You must not have a free press; why? That free press might disturb somebody. You must not have free schools; why? The free schools might reach this great multitude of poor white men, and by giving them enlightenment and instruction, they might see the gag that we have been keeping on their mouths in the past years. In fact you must have nothing free but *we*, the aristocracy of the South, the chivalry of the nation. You must not elevate the poor man to a higher scale of good. The South loves to cast its chains around the poor, and enthrall both black and white men, building up on this lower stratum of society, an aristocracy of self-styled chivalry, having for its motto the degradation and bondage of the black man.

"I know you would not have talked so plainly three or four years ago," says some one. If they had behaved themselves and made the best of the circumstances of the nation, we would not have spoken so plainly yet of what all knew in the past to be facts. You knew them, and I knew them for ten or fifteen years, and everybody knew them, but we wanted the house to be quiet.

Let me show you a specimen of this. About five years ago I stepped into a store in one of our Western states. It was just after an election that had gone Republican (as a good many things are going now-a-days). (Laughter and applause.) A gentleman from Kentucky, who had been dealing largely at that house, came into the store and spoke to the proprietor—came in as Southern gentlemen generally do, quite pompously in style. Said he, "Mr. Smith, (that was the name actually) (laughter) I wish to make a purchase to-day, but before doing it I wish to ask a question with regard to this house; I wish to know how many of this house voted on the Republican side at this recent election?" Well, Mr. Smith thought that was coming to the point, and he replied, "Mr. ——. I would like to inform you sir, that it is none of your business how many men in my house voted on the Republican side of this question." (Applause.) "But," said the Southern gentleman, "Do you know, sir, who I am?" "Of course I do," said Smith. "I am a gentleman from the South, who has dealt largely with you in the past, but am determined to deal no more with you, until this question is answered: *all* we Southern gentlemen resolved to deal with no house that patronizes that side of the question." "Well, sir," said Mr. Smith, "I think the time has just about come when *we* Northern gentlemen ought to tell *you* Southern gentlemen, exactly what we Northern gentlemen think of you, and have been thinking of you in all the past. We are men of trade, that buy and sell to get gain; we have bought and sold to you to get gain, and so long as you dealt simply upon principles of business, we could deal with you; but now, sir, the time has come when the film is torn away, and we wish you distinctly to understand, that *we* Northern gentlemen *know* you Southern gentlemen, and hereafter neither you nor any other of the South, can have goods from this house without paying down the cash." (Applause.) I saw that, and simply mention it as a fact, to show what we all knew; that in the past there was trouble in the family, there were some bad children in the house; but in order to keep peace we said nothing. Now the war has come and the South and North acknowledge the fact, and acknowledge it so as to prove to the world that one of the most powerful influences leading to the present Rebellion and disruption, has been that want of harmony, that absence of homogeneousness in these two sections of the country. Now since the war has broken out, Southern papers express their real sentiments.

The Richmond Inquirer, some few months after the rebellion commenced said, "We never were in sympathy with the Northern Democracy." It meant the Democracy in its good sense, for it has a bad sense. (Applause.) "We have never loved Republican institutions, we have never believed in the freedom of the people; on the contrary, we have believed in government, in law, in rule, in power, in subjugation, and we wish the world to understand that hereafter the Southern states lift up the cry, instead of liberty, equality and fraternity—slavery, government and submission." That is the spirit that has been in the South all along. One part of this country has had for its *beau ideal*, liberty, and has taken up in its true and noble sense, the motto of "equality, liberty and fraternity." Down in the depths of the heart of the other part, they have not dared in the past to use the cry, yet now, when they think they are free, they do use the cry of "Slavery, subordination, and bondage."

We all recollect that remarkable speech of Alexander Stephens, after he had made up his mind to cast in his lot with this terrible Rebellion. "In all the past," said Stephens, "we meant to lay as the foundation of our social life *human bondage*, and we must come out and boldly say that the corner-stone on which the Confederate States should be built, is that of human slavery." And yet I heard a gentleman say, not very long ago, that in Mr. Stephens' own house, in the year 1860, he heard Mr. Stephens say, that "whenever disunion takes place in this nation, our negroes will not be worth the salt we feed them."

What did this man mean? He was a noble and true man. He saw through it all, understood it all; but when the fatal die was cast, he simply chose to take his own share with the rest, and launched out in the full significance of rebellion, which he distinctly understood to mean subjugation, submission, and the thraldom of the lower classes.

I think, then, we have seen sufficient to show that I am not mistaken when I say that, lying at the foundation of the war, is the spirit, the customs, the habits, the wants, the institutions, and in a word the civilization of the two different sections of our country. This difference has had a large share in causing, and is the very foundation of, the Rebellion in which we are now engaged.

Some of you might ask the question—if what you say is true, had we better not separate? I would simply answer *no, never!* (Applause.) and next Tuesday night will give the reasons for my *no.* (Applause.)

Let us pass to the second. My second proposition, which I have stated as a cause that has led to this Rebellion, has been, the *growing political corruption that has entered into the government of our nation.* Our country, our government, national and state is corrupt, profoundly corrupt. In its forms, in its constitutions, in the laws, I believe it would be the best government that God ever gave to a people dwelling on this earth. In its administration, I believe for the past thirty years, it has been one of the most corrupt governments that the eye of God could look down upon on the face of this globe.

We had like all other nations in our infancy our Golden Age, our time of Republican purity, the days of our fathers when men pursued honest legislation, when statesmen and members of our legislative bodies felt that their business was to minister to the true welfare, to the real good of the nation; and we look back with just pride to these golden days of our nation's history. But I tell you, ladies and gentlemen, and you know it just as well as I do, that these things—simple, plain and pure, *" were forty years ago!"* I am going to make a statement that perhaps some will say is downright heresy : but it is a fact and I cannot help it. If I was to point to the time, when this political corruption first entered the country and began to breathe out its pestilence and death upon the nation, I would lay my finger on the year 1829 ; and though I dislike very much to say it, that is the year in which General Jackson became President of the United States. Now I know some will say that is heresy. "General Jackson? why he is the hero of the nation." So he is. "He is the idol of multitudes of the people." So he is; but I take it, we are here to study history. All honor to General Jackson for his glorious battle of New Orleans! All honor to this true patriot for defeating the base schemes of nullification in 1832! But we must stultify our senses and ignore the facts of our history before we can refuse to write alongside of this honor, the historical fact that the birthtime of the political corruption of our nation was in the administration of this very General. Go back now and look at our history, and up to that very time we can measure the Golden Age of our country. In the administration of his immediate predecessor, John Quincy Adams, we had as pure an administration as ever blessed this country ; and throughout the whole nation, North and South, there was peace and prosperity and virtue and unity and harmony, that reminds the reader of the golden days when such men as Washington and Jefferson, and the elder Adams themselves held the reins of our government. Every interest of the nation was prosperous. John Quincy Adams administered this government with men of all parties. He ignored no man for his political relationship. He exercised no power of his position to continue in office. He had nothing to do with that principle, " To the victors belong the spoils." Whenever he could find a good, true and honest man, whether he had been upon his side in the election or against him, he placed him in his cabinet or in the highest positions. The legislation of those four years was directed honestly and fairly to the welfare of the nation. I simply refer you to the history of the country to prove, that one of the proudest periods and noblest administrations, is that of John Quincy Adams, immediately preceding the year 1829. (Applause.) Now things are changed, sadly changed; and we need not go back to trace up the gradual unfolding of this change. The change, my hearers, was like a clap of thunder out of a clear sky. The change came instantly upon a people in the highest state of prosperity before 1829. Before 1833 came upon the nation danger, corruption, want, threatening poverty, anarchy, derangement of business and everything else deteriorated. What are the facts of the case ? One of the first acts of this earnest old General was a political proscription, putting out of every office every man on the opposite side ; the next was the establishment of a pensioned press, extending an influence that could not be seen or touched, and yet that was mighty and powerful throughout the whole nation. I say we can find in history that just at that time were born into the nation's life three of the most damning principles that ever entered into the administration of any government. I mean first that suicidal principle—" *To the victors belong the spoils.*" I mean secondly, that abominable principle, *that the administration in power must use the power of the government to secure its continuance in office.* I mean thirdly, that equally ruinous one, *that the legislation of our land must be directed toward the same end of perpetuating the power and the influence of the party.* Now I say just then the history of our country shows, were born those very destructive principles into our national life.

Look at the first one. Could it have been born anywhere else than in the depths of corruption—"to the victors belong the spoils!" The very sentence smells of blood, and looks like spoliation. Victors in a Republican government! " To victors," in a government for the administration of free institutions, "belong the spoils!" " We have won the battle, we have routed the foe, we have resorted to all means to gain the day, *the spoils are ours!*" What nation could live under a motto like this? No nation at all, and much less a Republican nation. Then it was born, and from that time to this it has been practiced, not by one party, but it has been accepted by all the parties of the land, and has become an unblushing, boldly announced cry of the politician, "To the victors belong the spoils." Men say it and do not blush! I wonder the Devil could say it and not blush! In a free country like this, in the midst of Republican institutions, "We have won the political battle, and the spoils are ours!" "Out with every man opposed to our party, cast him out of office," "direct all legislation to the continuance of ourselves in power;" and why? "We are victors and the spoils are ours!"

I have said this has entered into all the parties. When we had won the victory some two or three years ago, there was a little, insignificant position that a good Democrat had been occupying, I don't know how many years. I was desirous they should keep in place a good man, an honest man—worthy in every sense—well versed in the functions of the office. The whole community nearly wished him to be retained, yet because of this ruthless proscription, that has become the motto of the day, this gentleman was put aside, out of office. I thought I would call on a Senator from New Jersey in relation to this matter. I went and spoke to this man, telling him I thought it would be exceedingly pleasing to the Republicans as well as the Democrats, if this gentleman were allowed to continue in office. The Senator heard me quietly for a little while, listened to what I said, stroked his whiskers, and then without offering an argument said, "Well, Mr. Wiley, the 'spoils belong to the victors.'" (Laughter.)

What injury has this done in the nation! It has distributed corruption and pollution into all the political parties of the land; it has elevated men into office, the most unworthy to hold those positions. It has become definitely understood that the game played for in nearly every political campaign is but a game for spoils—that when victorious they may gather in the fruits. It is a contest for gold and power. It has excited strong political partizanship in our land. It has intensified the contests of these parties. I wish I could believe, and you wish you could believe, when we carry on a stern and intense political campaign for the election of President or Governor, that both parties were zealous to get the *best man* in the position, the best officers in power, the best laws passed. I wish in my heart I could believe it, and you wish you could believe it. We know it is not this patriotic desire to place the best men in positions, and to secure to the government the best legislation; but we know perfectly well, that the scheming, the plotting, the zealous efforts on both sides are, to get the positions for the rewards that are returned.

Passing to those other two principles, they are equally bad and destructive in their influence on the nation, Look at the legislative assemblies, look not far away from Trenton, when any subject comes before the Congress of the United States or the legislature of a single state, and see with what unerring accuracy you can tell how men are going to vote. You know the Republicans will vote on that side; and the Democrats will arrange themselves on that side. The vote is counted, and we are as familiar with it as with our a b c; it is a party vote. It is not a broad, patriotic, comprehensive view—is this measure for the welfare of the state or nation? It is not a broad patriotic and comprehensive view—is this a good law or is it an injurious one? But it is this—will it satisfy our constituents? How will this meet the wants of the party? How must I vote as Republican or Democrat? And when the vote is taken you can tell precisely how the two parties stand. What has been the consequence? Some of the basest laws ever passed by an enlightened nation, have been passed by our national and state governments; and some of the best laws, that would have administered to the welfare of the nation, have been cast aside, simply on the principle of a party vote like this. I say I wondered long ago that the God of heaven looking down on this nation, so dead to patriotism, so devoted to selfish gain and partizan politics, so reckless of the true interests of the nation and of the government, had not let his thunderbolt fall upon us long ago.

Some ask, "what has that to do with the Rebellion now upon us?" It has much to do with it every way. What is the Rebellion that is upon us? It is a partizan strife. It is one party that has been taught through all these thirty years, this lesson, that if you gain the victory you secure the spoils. It has been taught by this political corruption to struggle for the gain of mere official position, to hold the reins and rule and direct the affairs of the nation. It has disseminated political ambition. It has given rise to scheming and plotting in Congress and out of Congress. It has awakened the most intense party strife in the history of the past, and laid the foundation for that political aspiration for high positions in our land, that has taken full possession of one part of our country, "We'll rule or ruin." Who will rule or ruin? Men that love gold. Who will rule or ruin? Men that understand distinctly that if they gain the victory they are entitled to the spoils.

Who will rule or ruin? Men who see in the onward progress of virtue and righteousness and truth, that these abominable schemes are to be checked, the government taken out of their hands, and they are to be laid on the shelf. As soon as we reached a point in this political corruption when the integrity of the people said, "*this thing shall go no farther;*" as soon as we reached the point when we resolved to take out of the hands of the South the power of the nation, what was the result? Why they said, if we can't rule we'll *ruin.* What does it mean? It means the time has come when the South cannot rule the North, when it cannot have command over the treasury and government of the nation. It means the day has come when the people will elect honest men to fill the positions of the country, and will defeat those abominable principles that were originated thirty years ago. (Applause.) When these dishonest politicians south or north of Mason and Dixon's line found this time come upon us, they were ready to ruin rather than give up the spoils. We have a few north of this line as well as south. (Applause.) They don't like to see the spoils go out of their hands. They don't like the day to reach them when they shall no longer be able to dip their hands into Uncle Sam's pocket. (Laughter.) They don't like to know that a new class of men are to come, and try their hand in working this nation.

I say then in every way, in many respects it is this political corruption that has led to this disruption in our land. It is this that has awakened the spirit in the south—after the day of the dissolution of these men had come—to " let loose the dogs of war, and cry *havoc.*"

Let me call your attention to the third. I have stated it to be " *actual collisions occurring in the administration of our government.*" It was to be expected that in the administration of the government of a great country like this, with such separate and varying interests, with so many differing localities under that government, that we should have collisions and should have difficulties; but it was equally to be expected that we would always have wise and honest men who would be ready to meet these conflicts and guide the ship of state safely through them. Thanks to God's providence! we had these men—sterling, honest, patriotic men for many years in the history of our country, men whose names are indeed venerable and hallowed in the history of the nation—first among them stands the great Father of his country himself. (Applause.) Then such men as Jefferson, and Madison, and Monroe, and Clay, and Webster, men who have gone down to sleep in honorable graves, whose names our children will mention to the last generation upon our land. (Applause.) These men have passed away. It has been many a year since sterling and honest, upright and noble patriots like these stood in our congressional halls, and were ministers in our legislative assemblies. Heaven grant the day may soon come when, out of the multitudes of capable and honest and wise men throughout our once happy land, we shall select men not for their mere party services, not for their mere availability in an election, not for their mere purse that commands many votes, not for their mere political and party relationships, but for their might and power as patriots and as statesmen. I say, then, Providence having favored us with men like these during many years of our history, we guarded off these necessary collisions that came in the course of our government; but at last *one* came for which we had no wise hand at the helm, and the ship ran upon the rocks. (Applause.)

Let us look at a few of these collisions. The first was in 1819–20, it was the one usually called " the great Missouri contest," arising out of the admission of Missouri to membership in the Union as a state. At the session of 1818–19, the house of Congress passed a bill admitting Missouri into the Union, on the condition that all children born in Missouri after the passage of that act should be free when they reached the age of twenty-five, and no other means should be made use of for the introduction of slavery in the State of Missouri. The bill thus passed in the House, went up to the Senate, and was returned without the condition. The House refused to concede this point, and of course the bill providing for the admission of Missouri into the Union was laid on the table.

Congress adjourned, and the excitement that had already been awakened by the discussions in Congress, went out among the people. The first great contest, now more than forty years ago, arose on this question, the same that agitates us to-day. Flaming orators went through the North and the South discussing the slavery question, and the admission of Missouri into the Union. Conventions were called and agitated by this question. Legislative bodies acted upon it—the South taking the ground that Missouri should be admitted with slavery, and most of the northern conventions opposing the admission of a new state burdened with this institution. Thus matters stood in 1819 and 1820. It came up again before Congress. The House still stood upon its previous bill, that Missouri should be admitted on the condition that the children of her slaves should be liberated as they reached the age of twenty-five. The South took its ground broadly on what it termed the Constitution— that we, the government, had nothing to do with the status of slavery in Missouri, that it belonged to Missouri alone to settle that question.

The North took the ground, that as Missouri was not a state, it was in the power of Congress to say under what conditions she should be admitted into the Union. Then came the battle, the great contest that shook the nation to its center at that time, and there was raised even then—forty years ago—perhaps the first cry of the dissolution of the Union, and that cry came up from the same South that has been hurling it out on every critical occasion that has arisen in our country. There stood up one of the great men I have mentioned. He looked over this contest, and, as he said, "trembled at the danger that threatened." He threw himself between the parties and endeavored to pacify the elements and restore peace. That man was the illustrious Henry Clay! (Applause.) He came forward and stood in the breach between the two angered parties. He proclaimed himself as standing on the interpretation of the South. He stated it as his view that it belonged to Missouri alone to settle the question of slavery for herself, but then distinctly stated this, that so decided was his own antagonism to this terrible institution, that if he were a citizen of the State of Missouri, he would rather wish her to remain out of the Union, than come into it with this stigma and blot upon her. He went farther, and predicted, that while he thought in the abstract this was the right of Missouri, yet he lifted his warning voice and said to the South, "If in the coming time you insist upon this abstract right, and claim that the approaching territories that are coming into this Union shall have the power to enter into it clothed with this badge of infamy, you will inevitably bring a disruption of this Union." Then came the grand compromise of 1820. Missouri was admitted, admitted without the condition, the House yielding the point, on condition that the great northwestern territories should forever be dedicated to freedom. That contest was safely over.

We passed on till 1832. Then we had another—the great Nullification Contest—when this little lady from the South said she would not submit to the laws passed by the Congress of the United States with regard to the Protective Tariff; and when that stern old Unionist General Jackson, heard of it, he said if she did not submit, every foot of the soil of South Carolina should be covered with her own blood. That was about the right way to talk. (Applause.) It is a strange thing when we go back to study the history of that contest, to find that the first bill for the Protective Tariff was introduced by a Mr. Lowndes from South Carolina, and that the bill was advocated most strenuously by Hon. John C. Calhoun, the father, perhaps the true father, of Secession in our day, and a very little while after the leader in the great Nullification Contest.

The Protective Tariff became necessary by the war of 1812. In 1816. Mr. Lowndes of South Carolina brought forward his bill, and, after various successive modifications, we had a well-established Protective System about 1824. I might remark, it is just as strange when Mr. Lowndes brought forward this bill that the Republicans of New England and Massachusetts went strongly against it. Why? Then New England was not quite so large a manufacturing place as now, but her great interest lay in the carrying trade, in the boating and shipping business, and this tariff touched that a little, and therefore New England stood against it. In the course of fifteen years things turned round. The staple of the South, she saw, was cotton. She saw she could afford to sacrifice wheat, corn, everything else, to raise this staple and export it abroad. She saw that this manufacturing skill in the North, that has become so mighty, was then slowly developing itself to meet the wants of the country. She discovered this fact, that after she had sent her cotton abroad, and England manufactured it into goods and it was brought back to this country again, she was paying a tariff on her own product. She said, " I wont do it," and came up to the session of 1832 and said, " we must have an end of this Protective Tariff system, and we will not pay duties on our own goods." New England found then that her great interest lay in manufactures—that the South could raise their cotton or other staples, but that by her own mighty head and skilful hand she was compelled to make her fortunes. She stood up against this. South Carolina, who led off in this contest, said she would not submit, and claimed the power of every state in the Union to nullify at its pleasure the laws passed by the Congress of the United States. General Jackson listened, and said it was *not* the power of one state to nullify the acts of Congress. He issued a proclamation ordering South Carolina to obey the laws of Congress. He ordered soldiers into the state. The navy began to gather into Charleston harbor. Yet the proud little Miss stood up boldly, held a convention on the 19th November, 1832, in Columbus, and passed an ordinance there that the State of South Carolina was an independent and sovereign state, and that it was her power, and she would claim it and maintain it to the last, to nullify the acts of the Congress of the United States. That ordinance passed by the convention was brought into the legislative body of South Carolina, and they passed it, and laid down the test-oath that every officer of South Carolina, military and civil, should pledge himself upon oath to render his first allegiance to South Carolina, and to stand for the independence of his state. She threw out also a broad hint, that application would be made to Great Britain for aid in this contest.

You see how she still looked to England! In every emergency she has been sighing for these flesh-pots of England. The General stood firm; but both agreed finally to a compromise.

Again I must say something about General Jackson. He did what every good, honest ruler would have done—he did what I wish in my heart James Buchanan had done. (Laughter and applause.) But there was this difficulty in the case of General Jackson; he was ready to yield the whole ground to the saucy South, and was in sympathy with the movement of the South, and wished the overthrow of the tariff principle. He would have given up the whole ground, had not that same patriot come forward again, Henry Clay, and with the wisdom of a statesman pacified the contest (applause), saving the Protective System and satisfying the South by laying aside, for the time being, the tariff on all those manufactured articles which came into competition with the manufactures of our own country. That storm was over, and we have little idea now, except as we study the history of those times, how nearly that conflict came to realizing a rebellion in our land. South Carolina was armed and ready for the battle; and who for one moment doubts, if she had struck the blow, she would have been followed by her sister states of the South. Timely wisdom, honorable statesmanship, true patriotism, stepped forward and saved the wreck.

We had another collision. I would date it about 1844, continuing until 1850, or perhaps I might say, continuing to the present day; for it is the same struggle—originating about that time—that has thrown us into this contest.

When we go back to about 1840, or even back to 1832, we find the South had learned the fact that its interest was in cotton. It discovered the fact that cotton is a powerful exhauster of the soil, and must have increasing territory, into which it may move itself, that it may continue profitable and advantageous. There lay just west of this fertile South, now nearly exhausted, one of the most beautiful tracts of land on the continent. It was the territory of Texas. Into that country Southerners began to move by emigration, and about 1836 they had already poured into the minds of those native Texans the idea of their independence, and striking for liberty from the government of Mexico. The Texans liked the idea, and in 1836 proclaimed their independence, the result of which was war. The Texans obtained help from this country, principally from the South, but largely too from the North. I had personal friends, I remember—you had some, perhaps—to enter into this contest of the " *lone star* " for her independence from Mexican rule. Our country was hasty in coming forward to acknowledge the independence of the struggling Texans; and I have sometimes thought that during this contest, when we' have said so many hard things against France and England, we do not remember how soon, how offensively hasty, we were to recognize the independence of that state before Mexico had yielded the contest. In recollecting this, we might hesitate in some of our charges against these nations abroad. However, Texas gained its independence, and the great question came forward then, as she stood out alone, whether she should be admitted into the Union. The North strenuously opposed its admission. You recollect who was a prominent candidate for the Presidency then, Martin Van Buren, and you remember when the time came for selecting the candidate for the Presidency, Martin Van Buren, who was opposed to the admission of Texas, was set aside, and James K. Polk chosen, a man so little known that most of the people would ask, who is James K. Polk? Where did he come from? But who was pledged to the admission of Texas, and put in opposition against that noblest of patriots, Henry Clay. I still remember that contest. You recollect how the opposite party said one thing in Pennsylvania and another in Virginia. You remember how they cried "tariff and no Texas" when they came into the outside counties of Massachusetts, and cried "no tariff and Texas" south of Mason and Dixon's line. James K. Polk was elected President of the United States against the best known man, and one of the most honest patriots and wisest statesmen that our nation had ever produced. We know the people were largely opposed, in the North, to the admission of Texas into the Union. We understood, or our statesmen understood, that the admission of Texas as a state, already bound in perpetuity to slavery, would be laying the foundation of such a strife and contest in this nation that it would never end until it led to bloodshed and the destruction of the Union. Mr. Clay looked over the ground and gave us a prophecy that has been fulfilled to the letter. "I dread," said this statesman, "the day when Texas shall be admitted into this Union. It admits a precedent that will be pressed upon the nation until it can endure no more, then it will refuse; then will come the cry of disunion, and beyond that I dare not look." But Polk was elected, Texas admitted into the Union, and up came the old contest again with regard to her admission as a slave state. The battle was fought. Texas was carried in, slaves and all. A large territory, big enough for five states, was thus carried into the Union, and slavery established forever there, until we shall wipe it out. (Applause.) Then came a war costing $200,000,000. But we could well pay for that, for we got two big slices out of the Mexican territories, and gained the vast gold mines of California, and that rich silver district of New Mexico. Again came the encounter. What about? These states. The South said, "Here is territory free that must be slave." "No," said the North, and again came the contest, and battle that was finally ended by excluding forever out of California, and nearly excluding out of Mexico, this introduction of the badge of infamy, and throwing to the angry lion the crumb of that new fugitive slave law of 1850, which makes every Christian man's heart shudder and recoil, when he thinks that by any law of his native land he should become a hunter and catcher of his fellow man in bondage! (Applause.) It was not a large enough loaf to throw to the excited South. It was an outrageous doctrine to make every northern man a slave catcher! The people muttered and murmured, and the thundering continued in the nation from that day until this. I must give you another little episode.

About this time, when we thought the compromise of 1850 had brought a little peace into the country, there was born a new giant, some of you may remember his name, "Native Americanism"—he was called sometimes, "Know-nothingism." The young fellow grew rapidly and mightily, and began first to elect local officers, then to put in governors of states, and by the year 1854, he gave a pretty plain indication that in the contest of 1855 he would elect a Know-nothing President. There was a Know-nothing President elected in that year. (Laughter and applause.) But he did not belong technically to that class or party. It was a clear case as politicians looked over the field, that if something was not done to put withs around this giant, or crop the hair of this growing Samson, there would be a Know-nothing President in 1856. The giant arose and struck the Democracy at one of its weak points, and gave the contest the popular aspect of putting the nation on its guard against the mighty influence of the foreign element that that party had been securing. I think no statesman, no historian, on looking back over these times could doubt the question, that if that giant had been allowed to go on he would have made the next President, and established the new party. But now good and wise politicians and statesmen began to look over the ground and said, "This wont do. What shall we do? We must strike a new issue. We cannot go into this approaching campaign of 1855 on the issue of Native Americanism and Democracy. What shall we do? We shall strike a new issue." A new issue was struck for the people. There was introduced into Congress that bill that proposed to repeal the Compromise of Missouri of 1820, around which the memories of the nation, as a great pacificator, had been clustering for more than thirty years. Stephen A. Douglas the keenest politician we have had in modern times, saw exactly where to strike this nation's heart, and when he and his compeers brought forward, in the Congress of the United States, the famous Kansas and Nebraska bill, that proposed to throw open the territories of these United States to the ingress of slavery, *the watchword of the Rebellion was spoken.* Whether those men, by their political manœuvring, meant simply to throw out a new startling issue before the people of this nation, and thereby defeat this young giant; whether they looked forward in the dim future to see the coming storm they were to wake up, and saw this powerful agitation that was to move and stir the nation to an extent that no political exorcism in the future could put down; whether they foresaw it would inevitably result in rebellion and bloodshed and the cry of disunion, I don't pretend to say; but history, when it comes to analyze the events leading to this Rebellion, will write down upon one of its earliest pages *the man that spoke the watch-word of Rebellion in this country was Stephen A. Douglas.* That watch-word was the Kansas and Nebraska bill, and the repeal of the compromise of 1820. (Applause.) It verily made a new issue that fixed the heart of this nation, north and south. Every man in the South lifted it up and said, "That is the true doctrine for us; all the territories open to the peculiar institution. Away with the compromises of the past!" The men of the North said "No! not one step farther for this shame of the nation. (Applause.)

A new party sprang into power, a young giant, full-grown at its birth, with teeth in its mouth. (Applause.) This party nominated for its candidate—I admit on partizan or sectional grounds—John C. Fremont. (Applause.) The latter party took up just as sectional a candidate for the Presidency though born in the North, and the North has not felt very proud of him. (Laughter.) The contest waged was a battle for the Kansas and Nebraska bill and the repeal of the Missouri Compromise. It was a question of slavery in the territories of the nation. But Buchanan was elected, the bill was passed, the Compromise was gone, Kansas was open. The most terrible chapter of blood and mutual slaughter that our nation had ever had in its history before, was written upon the plains of Kansas. Four years of the most corrupt, imbecile, extravagant and traitorous administration our government had ever known, passed then; an administration when beneath the very 'eye, if not with the collusion of the President himself, treason was practiced and matured and ripened into life. The South distinctly understood from the time of that contest—the Toombses, the Davises, the Yanceys, the Tulees—all saw that the contest sprung upon the nation in 1855, in

1859–60 would win upon the side of liberty, right and the law; and it was a foregone conclusion they must separate and divide. The Southern papers spake it out clearly, conventions announced it distinctly—James Buchanan was to be the last President of the whole United States. During those four years, I say, everything was done, distinctly and avowedly, to prepare for this contest. Men occupying positions in the Cabinet itself were traitors, scattering our armies, sending off our navy, distributing into the South arms and munitions of war—practicing those arts of treason beneath the very eye of the President himself. Oh! what a blot on the history of this nation will be those four years of the administration of James Buchanan. Now another campaign came, and we must have new candidates for the great struggle of 1860. The Republican party laid down its platform. It was a platform that had for its most prominent principle the exclusion of slavery from the territories of the United States forever; and selected for their candidate honest Abraham Lincoln. (Applause.) A convention to elect a candidate for the opposite party met in Charleston, and from the commencement it was evident that there were two parties on hand; a Northern party, ready for the same old Douglas platform of the previous four years; ready to make every concession that could be made to this Moloch of Slavery, whose thirst was so great that nothing would satisfy it, but the free access and ingress of slavery to all the territories of the United States. Even the Democratic party could not swallow that, and the convention voted, one wing nominating Stephen A. Douglas, a man who has gone to render his account to God. The old logical saying, *nil de mortuum nisi bonum*, I would apply to Mr. Douglas, a true and honest patriot I freely believe in my heart; a man that meant well to his country, I have not a doubt, notwithstanding what I have said above. I am only sorry it was not in the counsels of the Infinite One to leave him for us in this contest. We would have found him heartily on the side of the government and of the Union, and his powerful influence might have told mightily in this struggle. He has gone to his reward and to his portion.

Another party bolted, but met again in preliminary convention at Richmond. (Laughter.) They laid down a new platform, and reassembled in Baltimore to establish their new creed by the nomination of Breckinridge and Lane. Then we had three parties in the contest. Let us look for a moment at the platforms offered to the American people. It was the contest that brought on the Rebellion. You will find the dividing line of all was the simple position they took with regard to the status of slavery in the territories of the United States. Said the Republican party, "Slavery must not be extended any farther into the territories of the United States—Congress has the power to limit it." Said the party of Mr. Douglas, and of that platform, "Leave the question of slavery alone to be settled by these territories themselves, and after they have settled it, and come up to Congress asking for admission into the Union, it is the simple duty of Congress to admit or reject: Congress has no power over the matter." Said the Breckenridge and Lane platform—the extreme Southern platform, "Slavery is entitled to its position and place in all the territories held as the common property of the United States, and Congress has the power and owes the duty, to guard and defend it in its introduction into these territories.

The three parties took their grounds. It may appear to some that the party that ought to prevail was the middle party, the one that proclaimed what might be called a compromise. We have the saying, "*in medio tutissimus ibis,*" safety lies in the medium; avoid extremes and you have the safe course. I admit here was the medium. There was the Republican party, saying "No slavery in the territories at all;" there was the other, the extreme Southern party, saying "Slavery in all the territories if we can put it there;" and there stood the medium party saying, "Let it alone, if the North can keep it out of the territories it is best, if the South can put it into the territories, all right." That seems like occupying the middle ground. I voted for the first one, for the platform of the Republican party, and you have a right to ask the question, why not follow then the old adage? Would it, not have been wise to have taken that middle ground which would probably have pacified both parties? I answer I had read with tears in my eyes the terrible history of Kansas. I had seen this experiment of "letting it alone." The nation had been groaning for four years under the cries of suffering men in this far western state as the North was trying to make Kansas free, and the South to make Kansas slave, and I recoiled, and tens of thousands, yea millions of voting freemen of the North, recoiled from the thought that Nebraska should be a Kansas, and Utah should be a Kansas, and New Mexico should be a Kansas, and every coming territory and developing future state of our country should be a Kansas, drenched with blood, baptized with the slaughter of its own children, before it should come into this Union. That is what the platform meant, and that is why the parties arranged themselves side by side, understanding distinctly there was no compromise when they had reached these two extremes. They intended somebody should win, and they knew who would be elected. The South meant that the Republican party should succeed, and Abraham Lincoln be President of the United States. It was a success, and Abraham Lincoln was elected; and now the idea of secession, disunion and separation came up all over the South. The die is cast, we can live no longer with the North.

On the 20th December, 1860, before any act whatever had been passed by Congress, and long before Mr. Lincoln had been inaugurated, South Carolina unfurled the banner of Rebellion. Congress assembled, bills were offered to pacify the South, compromises were presented, nothing was accepted. The same Mr. Douglas now came forward like an honest patriot, and took his stand on the side of the Union, and said to the man who is now the President of the Southern Confederacy, "Mr. Davis we can get for you, without a difficulty, the Crittenden Compromise;" said Mr. Davis, "We will have no compromise, we mean to separate." They were yet as you understand distinctly, in both houses of Congress, in power, and might have passed any laws or any bills of concession; and with a little trembling and misgiving, many a Republican too in that Congress would possibly and probably have gone over when the coming storm was in the future. No, it would not do. A peace convention was called. The best and wisest statesmen of the North and South met to devise measures to make peace. They offered the Crittenden Compromise; you remember what it was—"We will give you all south of 36° 40', and all you can get besides on the southern side of that line was implied in it—will that suit you?" "No," said a prominent leader in this Rebellion, "If you were to get us a *carte blanche* on which to write our conditions we would write nothing; we mean to separate." On the 7th day of January, 1861, Senator Tulee of Florida, wrote to his constituents from Washington, in these words—"I send to you herewith a report of the doings of a meeting of southern representatives, representing the States of Florida, Alabama, Georgia, Louisiana, and Texas, held in this city last night, to take into consideration the best means of separating from this Union. We agreed that it was best for the Southern States to separate, and that the separation should be made on or about the 14th of February. We put it off thus into the future to enable Louisiana and Texas to join with us." Signed by fourteen Senators, representing seven Southern States. You remember South Carolina was already out. How that reads like the doings of the celebrated Convention of 1790, in bloody Paris! How that reads like the history of Catiline and his co-conspiritors eighteen centuries ago! Fourteen Congressmen of the United States sitting by day in January and February of 1861, sitting by day in the halls of Congress, plotting to separate from the Union, and in spite of all efforts of the administration to stay the coming storm, at night retiring to their silent caucuses to develop more securely still their schemes of disruption and rebellion! Oh! that we had had in that day a Cicero for these Catilines! Oh! that we had, as Rome had, its dark chamber beneath the capitol into which the traitor entered, but out of which no man ever came. (Applause.) The die was cast. State after State seceded from the Union, fort after fort was taken, arsenal after arsenal was robbed, mint after mint, and the property of the nation appropriated to the use of the Rebellion. Major Anderson moved from Moultrie into Sumter—promptly Carolina moved into Moultrie. The Star of the West on her pacific voyage to feed hungry men entered the harbor of Charleston, and the first gun of the Rebellion was fired upon this peaceful messenger, and all this before a single man had been called by the newly elected President, all this before the 4th day of March, 1861! All what? Why the South had seceded, the Southern Confederacy organized, Jeff. Davis inaugurated, thirty thousand men called for, a pacific vessel fired upon by the traitors, fort after fort, naval position after naval position seized upon by these men, and then at last, though the President was inaugurated and gave out his pacific proclamation, determined to adhere strictly to the platform on which he had been elected, though the North stooped even to pusillanimity again to make friends with these men, at the last the emergency came, and our noble heroes of Sumter were starving. Again our proposals peacefully to give them food on which to live were refused. " No," said the men, " we must have war."

The President of the Southern Confederacy, on the 11th of April, " cried havoc, and let loose the dogs of war." It was done to fire the heart of the South, and *it fired the heart of the North.* (Applause.) An indignant people now endeavored to crush the Rebellion beneath the hand of the government. Mr. Lincoln called for seventy-five thousand men, and thirty-five thousand more were called for by Davis. This is the beginning of the struggle. Yet said these men, " you *drove* us into the war." After making every preparation and every arrangement to strike the first blow, against every concession a free, and generous, and noble people could make, yet these miserable traitors and their sympathizers in the North say, " You pressed us and left us nothing but battle and war !"

You ask now, in conclusion, " how we got into this war?" Two people differing in spirit and aspirations, two societies differing in their civilization have come at last, after slow and long development, into an actual conflict of arms ; a conflict that perhaps no human wisdom could have prevented. One or the other of two antagonistic civilizations as these must be crushed, for both cannot live together. Do you ask what brought us into this conflict? I answer the corruption that was spread throughout all our land, the defection of politicians from the true principles of national government, and the consequent ministering to party schemes and partizan interests. You ask what led to this struggle? I answer chiefly, and above all, *slavery* is the heart, the spirit, and the soul that lies at the bottom of all the causes I have mentioned before. (Applause.) Why are we a different people and have a different society and spirit and civilization? Because in the North we are free, and in the South they hold their fellow-men in bonds. Why have we become profoundly politically corrupt in the past? I answer; because there was one section of our country that had an immediate interest incorporated with its life, around which it rallied all its power, over which it threw its whole guardian care, and for which it bought the votes of the nation to sustain it in existence. What has brought these collisions that I have mentioned in the past? I answer since 1820 *it was slavery ;* in 1832 *it was slavery ;* in 1844 *it was slavery ;* in 1850 *it was slavery ;* in 1855 *it was slavery ;* in 1860 *it was slavery.* It was the corner stone of the Confederacy. In the first speech of the Vice-President, of that *non-descript*, the cause of the war is represented to be that institution which has nursed its spirit in the South, and has awakened opposition in the North.

We are in war. Why? Because the world moves, because society grows, because Christianity advances, because the earth, in each cycle it makes, sloughs off a mass of sin and hell, and rolls onward toward that brighter day, when heaven and earth in peace shall meet and kiss each other. (Applause.) Why are we in war? Because the world has grown too old to be blotted any longer by slavery. Why are they in Rebellion? Because Christianity has gone so far that the time has come to cry *liberty* to the bondsman. (Applause.)

Slavery then, we answer, and the recoil of human nature against this system, has been the spirit, the life and the soul of this Rebellion. "No," says some man, "it was you Yankees." (Laughter.) "It was you Northerners. You would not let slavery alone." I don't agree with you. I don't believe that that caused the Rebellion ; but if it did, if you are right in that opinion, it simply proves what I have said. It is a very clear case that the Yankee would not have talked about a thing if it had been *non est.* If there had been none of this evil, it would not have stirred the heart of Christianity, not simply in Yankee-dom, but through the whole North—throughout the whole world. I admit that speech-making, book-writing and sermon-preaching had much to do in awakening this contest. I admit that the world is moving onward in its march toward better things, and that stirred the hearts of the men who felt guilty in their consciences of a wrong against humanity. Why didn't they keep still? Because they could not. Why didn't Peter and John keep still when the Jewish Sanhedrim said, "speak no more or we will give thee stripes and imprisonment." Said Peter and John, "we cannot but speak the things we have seen and heard." Put down the voice that speaks against this oppression and wrong? Dam up the Niagara; stop the already exploding volcano; hurl back the flashing lightning, and then talk of this advancing spirit of humanity, and command it to be still in the presence of this human wrong! Only a little while ago in this advancing spirit of the age, Russia offered deliverance to her serfs, and shall we in this great country, whose pride is liberty, and which God has made the palladium of human rights, shall we keep still and let this gigantic wrong grow and spread and prosper in our land? No. (Applause.) You ask too large a price for the privilege. What is it? Some few families, at the utmost measurement some three hundred thousand men, in the South, cried out "let us alone, we must have these bondsmen, it is our institution, it is our right." Mark it! three hundred thousand men, women and children, perhaps some ten thousand families have this claim on these millions of men they are holding in bondage! And now what price do they ask? They say to the world, "stop your free press; close up your free schools; silence your free church and pulpit; away with all these utterances of evil and these cries after the welfare of humanity; stop the car of human progress; stay the onward march of Christianity; hold back the course of civilization itself!" Why? Why shall I not speak from my sacred pulpit the counsel of God? "Because I want to hold slaves." Why shall I chain the free press of America and distort its utterings? "Because I (this little minority of humanity) wish to hold slaves." Why must Christianity distort itself, and misrepresent itself, and become corrupt, and bow, and cringe, and stoop, and stay its onward progress of triumph, why? "Because I wish to hold slaves." Admit your ground is right, that it is the onward progress of liberty and right that has brought on this collision between the two sections of our country; then it still is true, that slavery lies at its foundation. I don't believe that that is its cause. It has been mighty; but tenfold more mighty has been that degeneracy of society, that corruption of the community; that hardening of hearts, that searing of consciences, that development of a thirst for gold, that ambition for lawlessness and aristocracy, that is the fruit of slavery itself, that has led us into this conflict.

With these remarks, I thank you for the patient hearing you have given me. I have talked longer than I thought to have done. I have presented to you what strikes me as the causes of the present Rebellion. I have tried honestly to answer the question, "How we got in?" If some of my facts as I have stated them are new, they are the results of patient study and examination. If some of them cross your prejudices, it is not a time for prejudice when a nation trembles in the balance held up by its God. It is not a time for prejudice when weeping widows and desolated houses are saddening the whole North and South. Away with all these prejudices, and look fairly in the face of the facts, and see the black and damning cause that has led this nation steadily on until it has plunged us into bloodshed and war. (Applause.)

HOW TO GET OUT.

I shall have to crave your indulgence again this evening with a few personal remarks. You have already discovered that I am quite hoarse. I should much better, I presume, be at home in bed, than attempting to speak to-night; yet I think if you will allow me to talk a little carefully at first, until I get my vocal organs warmed up and ready for operation, I shall be able to continue the lecture of the evening.

I have come, then, such as you find me, and shall try to do the best I can in presenting the thoughts of the evening on the subject announced for the lecture—"How to get out of the war."

We tried to direct your attention on last Tuesday evening to "How we got into the war," and we did so because we think it essential to getting out that we rightly understand how we got in. As a practicing physician for a number of years, I learned that it was very important in coming to visit a patient to find out what was the cause of the man's disease, especially if it was a cause within himself or that was constantly operating, in order to relieve him from his malady; and when I had found out that cause, I had gained so much towards his cure. I recollect about a year ago at a meeting occupying the platform in the city of Philadelphia in connection with another gentleman. We were speaking on the subject of the war. He was a peculiar kind of War-Democrat, and friend of the war and government, and had a great deal to say about these "hot Republicans," and about the reverence that was shown to the negro and to slavery, and used one of the most powerful sentences I think I ever heard in showing the absurdity of paying any attention to the cause of this Rebellion. I felt a little warm while I was sitting behind him, and listened to his remarks pretty decidedly, not knowing exactly where I could hit him, until he finally made use of an illustration. It was this:—"What would you think of a physician who came to attend a man with a cold, who would begin to examine his boots, and on finding that his cold had come from his having a hole in his boot, to cure the man, would order the boot to be mended? Would not that be absurd?" Perhaps it would; and yet there are some occasions in which the mending of the boot, although it might not cure the cold that

(32)

he already had, would have a decided effect in keeping off the next. (Laughter.) I thought I had the advantage, and could give a better illustration. You see his illustration was simply a special one to apply to a general subject. I took as my illustration a general one, that led its application to a general subject such as the Rebellion is. I called the attention of the citizens of Philadelphia to the condition of their streets, their sewers and alleys, and said, suppose there was a fatal disease ravaging this city, sprung evidently from the corruption and filth collected in your streets and alleys, would there be anything absurd in removing these filthy accumulations in order to stay the ravages and progress of this disease? And the audience saw my illustration was best, and took him down and put me up. (Laughter.)

Before I take up the question—"How are we to get out of the war"—I would like to consider it in a negative form, and show how *not* to get out of it. I think that during the past two and a half years we have had not a few people in this country that are not particularly anxious to get out of the war, and decidedly prefer to continue in, especially in some quarters where it is a paying operation, or with some because it makes political capital; some especially who would wish the war to continue at least during the year 1864. You can contribute very considerably towards the perpetuity of the war upon us by being a *peace man*—always talking about the pleasures of peace, always referring us back to the halcyon days that we had before the war came, complaining terribly about the taxes that this war is bringing upon us, talking about the loss of our liberty, the terrible tyranny and oppression of our government. To perpetuate this war, do everything you can to make the community in general believe that the country is going to be ruined. If you are down in the lower walks of life, oppose everything the government undertakes to do. A capital thing to oppose is the draft. If the government calls for men to sustain itself, don't go yourself, and don't let any other man go if you can help it. If you are not a pious man, swear a little, curse the negro, say all you can against this downtrodden and persecuted race. If you are an editor, you have a large field and much better opportunity for carrying out this idea. If you are an editor, bring out a leading editorial in every paper against the absurdity of the measures of the government. Convince the people that read your paper the government is wrong. Give them to understand that if you were placed at the head of the administration you would soon bring the war to a close. But the best capital you can make is by speaking of the tyranny of the government. Convince the people they are losing their liberty, so that every man who reads your paper can see while you are complaining about the curtailment of liberty you have gone yourself into Jacobinism and libertinism. If you are in the legislature, you are in a capital position to continue the war for several years to come. Make the legislation of simple bills that for three readings would last three days, make them last all the winter. Divide yourselves off into strict party votes. Insist on everything that shall be made to bear on the interest of your party, that a measure shall be popular or unpopular, just as it promotes the interest of the party platform on which you stand.

When the government comes forward to ask for men, use all the legislation you can command against it. Become terribly afraid about the independence and sovereignty of the individual states. Be greatly alarmed for the honor of his excellency the Governor, for fear he should lose his dignity. Get up a bill to keep the soldiers at least two miles away from any polls of an election. (Applause.) Be sure that on no account you allow the soldier to have a vote, for he is generally likely to be a loyal and true man, and true to his country. (Applause.) If you are Governor of a state, you are in a capital position to continue the war for an indefinite period to come. Get out your flaming message every time the legislature meets. Put in your message the most ridiculous and absurd distortions of all that has been done the previous year by the administration. Be remarkably strict in standing on your dignity as Governor of the State. If there should come a draft in your state, be particular about the number of men; be sure to count the enlistments under your administration, so that you see how many men have been taken; if you make a mistake of seventy thousand men, it don't make any difference, it delays the government. Make the humbler classes believe they are persecuted, that they are awfully burdened by the grandest tyranny that ever came into the world. Excite them under the idea of the persecution that has come upon them in the form of a draft. If you get them so excited that they begin to gather in mobs in the streets, if they begin to kill men and destroy property, and make a new Rebellion, don't be scared, just go in among them and call them *friends.* (Applause.) If you can get in Congress, you have a fine opportunity to delay the operations of the government, and to continue the war. I need not delay you long on the chances you would have in this position, because we have had some capital examples. There is Vallandigham. You can follow in the footsteps of Breckinridge during his brief congressional administration. You can follow Burnett of Kentucky, or his patron from the same state, Davis, and oppose everything that tends to a vigorous prosecution of the war. Insist upon it that the most profound respect and reverence shall be paid to the property question. And here permit me to say, that of all the absurd things that has come before my mind in this war, nothing has made me feel smaller as an American than this same property question. Read over the doings of the legislature and Congress, and you would think that property was truly the great Deity of the American people. The right of all rights, the sacred thing above all sacred things. And no matter in what form that property is found, whether it is real and immovable estate, or movable estate standing on two feet, it is the same thing. You may take men, you may protract the war, you may shed seas of blood, but don't touch property. Stand on that ground as you stand on your life. No pity for the poor widow's son ; take him, no matter ; take the father's joy and hope, no matter; take the stay and support of a family ; let them all go ; but don't touch the man whose face is black ; don't touch a man whom another claims as property ; in fact risk the perpetuity of the Republic rather than lay your hand on the great ideal of human property. I am sick of this.

In reading over one of the speeches in Congress, made by a gentleman already named to-night, did you ever see anything more absurd than the ground taken by that gentleman on the paying-for-the-negro question? Now I don't care, nor do you care, whether or not the owner is paid for his slave ; but in this time of war, in this struggle for the nation's life, it does strike me as the most nauseating thing I have ever found in human history, that we may take all the white men for the service of the government, with not a word about pay, but must not touch a black man who is held in bondage—must sacredly observe the bonds of this poor wretch. The draftsman may go into your house and take the son, the hope of your future life, worth ten thousand slaves in your estimation, and who is to pay, or who dreams of asking the government to pay for this son of your heart's love, and of the care of years? Yet, if he enters into the Southern man's house, or into the border states, and lays his hand on this biped, the government may have him on the condition that he is paid for! The poor widow's son may be thrust into the army, and who talks about compensating or paying her for the use of her son? Yet the black man must be paid for because he is property, and the government must stoop from its high position assumed eighty years ago, and for the sake of this miserable principle recognize property in man. Where in the Constitution of the United States is ever recognized that principle? Throughout that sacred document, we have never yielded the point; our fathers were wiser men than that to recognize in a public document—the corner stone of our national government—property in our fellow man. The term the Constitution uses for these men is " persons held to service," and recognizes them distinctly as persons, and has always (permit me to say very unjustly) been allowing a large representation in the government of our country in behalf of these persons. And yet when these persons so noticed in the Constitution of the country, and so represented in Congress, are needed for the country's service, editors by hundreds and politicians by thousands, say the country has no right to touch this property, or to lay hold upon a man who is held as the property of another. It is just like that other absurd principle that has seemed so strange to me—the demand for recognizing the rights of traitors under the Constitution of the United States! You must not confiscate the traitor's property. Why? Property is something sacred and beloved in the American mind. Be careful of the traitor's Constitutional Rights. You must not hurt the traitor. Whip him *easy*, get him subdued *softly*, bring him back *gently*, leave him as well off when the war is done as when he commenced it; fight him with magnanimity, with philanthropy; but above all things don't hurt the traitor! Where in all the history of the world have we learned the fact except in America—a principle largely used by some men—that the traitor having gone out from under his government, thrown off his allegiance to the government, takes up arms against his government, grasping at the very throat and life of the nation, must have still preserved the Constitutional Rights that belong to him as a true and loyal citizan? My hearers, I read history, and I learn there is one right that belongs to a traitor. When a man lifts up his arm to shed the blood of the country, he forfeits all rights but one, and that is the right to hemp enough to hang him. (Applause.)

Now look at the absurdity. The traitor has lost every right, even that of his life—and is not life the most sacred possession? Is it not the most valuable possession?—And yet here is the cry, "you must not touch his property nor harm anything that belongs to him." You must religiously conduct the war in such a way as to leave him as well off in the end as he was when he began. If you follow out this plan as citizen, as editor, as legislator, as governor, and as congressman, you can perpetuate the war for any indefinite number of years to come; and if any of you should happen to get into the position of general, then you have a capital opportunity. You have simply to gather your army together, take nearly one year to drill it; (Laughter) every other day have a grand review of a division, get everything ready to move, tell the country you are going to move, and then find out that the ambulances are not on hand. (Laughter.) Get the ambulances all ready, tell the nation you are ready now to move, then find out that you need thirty wagons to carry your baggage. (Laughter.) When the thirty wagons are made you can call in council your other generals, and conclude it is not time to move yet. (Laughter.) No matter if a higher power says move, you delay, and when you do move you will only have to battle with double-headed Dutchmen and Quaker guns. (Laughter.) What difference? You have delayed the war! Try it again ; strike out and take some new and unwonted course to find the goal—Richmond—and settle down before Yorktown, lose a good example (Laughter), and if there is only ten thousand men there so much the worse. If you have one hundred and eighty thousand or two hundred thousand men, what is the use of making a sudden attack on these men ; that would not be fair. (Laughter and applause.) Begin to lay siege to the town ; throw out miles of fortification, spend thirty days in front of these ten thousand men, and all the time throw out the idea that you are going to bag them. (Laughter.) When the thirty days are up and you have done the story of the bag, if the bag is empty so much the better; the ten thousand men will live to fight again. (Laughter.) Give the enemy abundant time to know you are coming, and never take him foul. Carefully guard his property, for that is sacred ; send a large number of your soldiers for this service, and be especially careful of biped property, which is movable. Continue this until the enemy is so fortified that he is too strong to take, and is likely to take you, then change your base. (Laughter.) It is an interesting operation. (Laughter.) If the enemy gets tired of this and attacks you, follow him at a respectful distance. If he corners you and you can't get out of it, fight him, and as you have good and brave soldiers you will whip him. But don't follow him too closely, that is ungenerous ; let him go over the river, give him a month to recover. If he be disheartened, and his army is broken, and you send him back howling into rebeldom, wait until he has recovered.

It is an easy thing to answer the question, "How *not* to do it, and how to continue the war." So many have practiced this interesting game, that a war that would not have lasted a single year, had the true strength of this country been exerted as the force of one man, has been perpetuated until the present time, and may be, should this continue, for years to come. But this will not continue. This whole class of men I have been referring to, have grown wiser. They find that all that kind of thing can be seen through, and that there is a vast amount of common sense in American society, and that while that game may be played upon them for a little while, we are apt to look the thing right into the eye and before long come to a just and honest conclusion; and Congressmen who act in this way soon go up to Canada or some other place. (Laughter.) Legislators of this kind don't go back; they board at home next winter. (Laughter.) Governors that pursue this course, don't find votes enough to reinstate them; generals that delay battles in this style quit before long and go into a business that pays better—making out presidencies. (Applause.) We bring in a new class of men. We have such men now as Grant. (Applause.) United States Grant. (Applause.) U. S. Grant. (Laughter.) Never Surrender Grant. (Applause.) Always Ready Grant. (Applause.) Uncle Sam Grant. (Applause.) That is the kind of men that knows how to do it, and that has never wasted his time in the miserable art how *not* to do it. We have a Meade—that is a very gentle drink to take in summer, but it will be *strong* Meade next summer. (Applause and laughter.) We have a Butler (applause) who has started out from the commencement just about right. He understood this war, because he helped to make it. (Laughter and applause.) He knew its character and spirit as well as any man knows his own child, but in this General Butler there is a great American spirit. When Jefferson Davis reported his determination to carry out Secession, said Butler, "Mr. Davis, we'll whip you to death if you do." "No," said Mr. Davis, "tho Yankees are cowards." "No," said Butler, "we'll annihilate you, and I'll be one to lead in the work." (Applause.) And he has been leading ever since. If you will give us a few more men after this stripe, that have no future prospects to look after, but have the only grand work in view of whipping out the Rebellion from our land, it will be but a short time until the mighty strength of the government will show itself in the conquest of her foe.

Now let us turn to the positive side of the question. We have seen enough how *not* to do it. All wars must come to an end, and must come to an end, too, by some agreement on terms reached between the belligerent parties; and we are all anxiously looking forward to the time when we shall see at least the coming of the end of this great contest. I think there are three ways of getting out of this war. I can conceive of no other than three. The first is by *separation;* by acknowledging the right of disunion, and submitting to the disruption of the Republic; and we have some who, of course, desire this result and are fighting for it; and yet it is altogether appropriate to specify who are the men who desire a disruption of the Union. When I turn attention to the North, I don't believe we have any class or body of men who are disunionists. I think we have some men as individuals, some emissaries of the South, perhaps hired and paid for their services rendered to the South, who are engaged in doing all they can to bring about a dissolution of the Union ; yet I have never for a single moment thought that we had any political party that desired this result in the North. I know that some people hastily charge on the Democratic party this intention, or state at least that the Democratic party would as leave see the Union disrupted as not to have it restored in their own particular way, and in such a way as would again give to them the government of our country ; but *I don't believe a word of it.* I do not believe that the Democratic party aims at the dissolution of the Union. I have never thought so for a single moment. I know that party is a great political affair ; I know it is exceedingly acute and far-seeing ; I know it has the best politicians in this nation ; I know they can lay their schemes a little wider, a little longer, and a little more accurately than any other political organization in the country ; they have been doing so for years, and are well skilled in the work. I should lose my confidence in the great Democratic party if it was not engaged in the same interesting business now ; if it were not in these great times looking forward to the future ; yet we can see no possible motive why any national party this side of Mason and Dixon's line should for a moment desire the disruption of this Union. The doom I think of the Democratic party would be written forever if the line of division was drawn upon that Mason and Dixon's line. They need the South ; they need the Southern influence ; and instead of desiring a final disruption of the Republic, they would aim at such a conclusion as will bring back again into the field this great political organization, the power and influence of the South. It is sometimes charged upon one wing of the Republican party, that they desire disunion ; and the only copperhead meeting I ever attended—I didn't intend to tell you that, (laughter) but I did attend one once, a very interesting one that was reported here in Trenton as a grand success. It was held up here somewhere a few miles above Pennington ; some two or three hundred were gathered together, and three very celebrated speakers were present. It was reported here next day as a grand convention of several thousands ! There were only about two hundred and fifty men women and children (laughter) at the meeting, it was charged upon one wing of the Republican party that they desired the disruption of the Union, and the proofs brought forward were the expressions of some radical men in the United States—that have been radical for years in the past and I presume are radical to-day—but who never in any single respect represented the Republican party. The men quoted were Wendell Phillips and William Lloyd Garrison, and many of their sayings, made a number of years ago, were brought forward to prove that the Republican party was aiming steadily and uniformly at the disruption of the Union. We know that some of these radical men a few years ago—and they may stand on the same ground this day—took this position, that "if there was no other way to correct the wrong of bondage to the black man—if there was no way to stop this terrible influence of a compact Southern oligarchy ruling over the nation, its politics and government, than by a disruption of the Republic, they were willing to see the Republic rent asunder, rather than this gigantic evil and these influences should continue in the nation." But I presume that all concede to the Republican party an honest intention to carry on this war to restore the Union. In the North I cannot think we have an element amounting to any strength that desires this war to terminate in disunion. When we pass South of this line we find disunionists. When we go back to trace the history of the war, we find even in the Southern country men who loved the Union. There were then two parties. In the first place—you must permit me to recognize humanity wherever I find it with the habiliments and the appurtenances of man—I say in the first place we have four millions of men in the South that certainly never desired the disruption of this Union; who felt that their future, their liberty, their welfare, lay in the continuance of this Union. Then we had a vastness in the South of what is called "white trash," or ignorant white people, who knew nothing and cared nothing about the Union. They were profoundly ignorant of the movements going on in the nation, and were only taught the one grand element of their creed, to hate the Yankee, and they didn't know why. Here is another vast class that had no interest in the disruption of the Union; and when the facts come to be known, perhaps there are but two states that honestly and truly voted themselves out of this Union.

Let us turn our attention to Louisiana; we have never had a report of the vote taken upon which the Act of Secession was passed. We turn to Tennessee, and the majority was against the Act of Secession. Texas was the same as Louisiana. Never to this day has there been a vote of the people. The slaveholders were tired of the Union and wished to retire from connection with this great government. There are three hundred thousand men, three hundred thousand slaveholders, that are the disunionists of this country; and it makes me feel sometimes exceedingly indignant when I see that in this nation of more than thirty millions of souls, three hundred thousand slaveholders, and even that number could be eliminated and reduced down to half of it, have risen up in this gigantic Rebellion, laying its foundation in wrongs, spreading its power in falsehood, distilling lies and perjury among the ignorant masses, awakened up so large a portion of all this country against the best government that God ever gave to men! (Applause.) We have, then, I say, about three hundred thousand people that are the prime movers—and this number can be reduced to one-half without any difficulty—who struggled for the disruption of this Union, and who perhaps still desire it. The other vast majority are still bound in their heart's love to the old stars and stripes, still love the memory of our fathers, still cherish one common history, still look forward to the permanence of our government, the palladium of human liberty, down to the evening of time.

We have other enemies who desire the disruption of this Union—enemies who have been working to bring about this end as one "most devoutly to be wished." We have an enemy to our republican institutions and government in England, and to the great principles and growth of our country, to the grand idea that man ought to be free, because he is capable of being free and governing himself. I say we find a great enemy to all these things in Great Britain, and doubtless long before this time, if it had not been for the hardy yeomen of that nation, the honest men whose hands are hardened with honest labor, the industrious mechanics who rank as we rank, who stand on the common level of humanity, and who understand what this great contest means, kept perpetually saying to the aristocrats of England, "No, this war is for human rights, for the perpetuation of free government, and you must not and shall not interpose." The aristocracy of England is against us. Only two weeks ago we read in the *Times*, the great organ of British aristocracy, an honest confession that, throughout its whole past career with reference to this country, it was moved by the one sole, pusillanimous thought that this nation was growing too strong, that it was getting to be too mighty a republic, and that it ought to be divided; that the interests of England demanded that this young giant should not continue to grow into such great strength.

Cross the channel again, and you find a subtle and keen enemy to our republican institutions in the "nephew of his uncle," whose only merit lies in his great relative, who would like to see the South prevail over the North ; who would then find a grand opportunity of carrying on his Mexican and south-western expeditions on this continent. There we find an enemy ; and there again, among the stalwart peasantry, we have friends by the thousands, who say, "*No*, no emperor and no aristocracy shall interfere with this young representative of free humanity that is growing up into a strong and gigantic life." Well may it be said, God is on the side of free institutions. Eternal right is on the side of this young republic. Humanity in its true and common impulses the world over is on the side of our government, and against the perpetuation of our republic no emperor, no aristocracy can carry out their designs in the face of feelings like these, while we do right and stand true to the destiny that God has ordained for us. (Applause.)

You see, then, after all, it is hardly worth while to discuss the question, Shall this Union be separated? Why should it separate? At the bidding of some three hundred thousand men who hold property in their fellow men? For the mere interests of England, that she may remain queen and mistress of the ocean, and continue to dictate to the nations? 'At the bidding of Louis Napoleon, that he may carry on his particular schemes of aggrandizement in the south-western parts of this continent? For whom should we disrupt this grand and glorious Union that the God of heaven gave our fathers, to descend to us and our children? No, never; never can we for one moment yield the point in settling this question by granting the secession of those who have risen in rebellion against the government.

We have men whose vigor and youth are passed away, who are terribly afraid of war, terribly afraid of taxes, and who would, at almost any price you can mention, buy the boon of peace, even saying to these men, as one said three years ago, "Erring sisters, go in peace." "*No*," I say, "erring sisters, *come back* and behave yourselves." (Applause.) Why can't we use this polite language and disrupt the republic? I answer—*First*, God never intended this continent to be divided into little petty governments; our geography and history indicate that fact plainly. Take down your map and look upon this fair province that God has given us. He has stretched out its streams, its lakes, and mountain courses, so that while emigration passes from East to West on lines of latitude, all the great streams of our country run from the North to the South. The mountain ranges extend from North to South. These streams carry the benedictions of the North to the extreme Southern shores. These range of mountains, with their solemn echoing, catch the voices of the North and sound them far down again into the South. Where, in the geography of the country, could you draw a dividing line? Nowhere has the God of Nature made barriers or reared division lines that would say, *"divide and here be thou separate."*

I say again, No, for not only does the geography of our country forbid it, but to admit the idea of secession would be to lay down for all future time that most suicidal doctrine in our country that as soon as one party is dissatisfied rebellion is the cure. If there is one natural barrier that would serve for a dividing line, it is the great Rocky Mountain range. Let us acknowledge the independence of the South, and in a few years more the interest of the great western countries might make it apparent to some that it would be better for them to separate from the government at Washington. No government can live under the doctrine of secession. When our fathers made the compact of union, it was made *perpetual*. It was intended as a permanent arrangement. They were not madmen. Who could for a moment suppose that men laying the foundation of a grand commonwealth could plant in the midst of this foundation an element that was to lead to the disruption and destruction of the nation itself?

We dare not accept this doctrine again, because it would not meet the occasion in settling the disputes between the two parties. I always thought that Wendell Phillips and Lloyd Garrison, and all that party, made a great mistake when they talked about disunion, and used to say they would rather see the country disrupted than that the Northern people should continue complicated with the great evil of the South. What would this do towards ending the difficulties? Could we live peacefully together as enemies, when we could not live together as friends? Could we not agree on the slave question when we were one, living under one constitution, one government? How, then, can we agree on this question when we should have drawn a line to separate the two sections? What terms could we make with regard to this slave question? We now consider this an independent country. We now have a foreign nation lying at our side. Grant them all they could ask, and lead back to bondage their liberated slaves, would you consent to be huntsmen for your fellow-men? And if you did, how long would it be before a nation, starting out in its rebellious career, would cease to be the sister Republic on our South, and would become what it aims to become to-day, a grand monarchy, frowning upon us from our Southern borders? Why those men are tickled to death by the idea of kingdoms, dukedoms, and earldoms. King Davis would sound mellifluously in the trumpet of fame. Earl Mason and Duke Slidell would be grand titles. (Laughter.) You smile at this; yet it is the inspiring thought of these men. "We are tired," said they, "of this *rank Democracy*, we are tired of this Republicanism. It is a failure." It was a decided failure with them; but we will teach them that it is not a failure, but that it is a power, and the most intense kind of power that can be concentrated for the government and perpetuation of the Union. I say we would soon have a monarchy at our side. My good old friend would then say, "Oh these horrible taxes," for there would be far greater taxes when the country would be under the necessity of maintaining a standing army of several hundred thousands, stretching along the border line between these two nations. You talk about the loss of life. There would be greater loss of life in the perpetual hostilities that would arise between these two portions of this nation. God never meant two people should occupy the country that is appropriated to this republican government, and no matter who those two people are, this continent, the whole boundless continent, is ours. (Applause.) No power can ever divide it. It is settled in the counsels of the Almighty. (Applause.) Civilization says *no.* A voice comes from the humble men of England, of Ireland, of France, and of all Europe, saying, "Never yield ground to this uprising of barbarism." Thousands of these men send us their letters, their commendations, their sympathies, telling us our interests are staked with yours, and humanity itself lies trembling in the balance of this great war. "You are fighting," say the noble spirits of Europe, "you are fighting not America's battle alone, but the battle of *humanity.* End it; *whip out* of your country this spirit of insurrection. Crush it, this wrong that has been a stain on your escutcheon all through your history; and in the future the God of heaven will smile upon you, and use you as He has ever intended to use you, as the center of a higher and nobler civilization." (Applause.) Disunion in this day, when the nations are moving forward to embrace each other in their arms! Disunion in America, this type and model of national life! Why, it is the last place on earth where any such principles should enter the minds of the people. Disunion here, when Europe is coming nearer together, and we seem to be nearing that time when nation will hail nation as its brother? Break up this grand Republic at a time when God in His mighty Providence seems rolling on events for the brighter and better days that shall acknowledge the brotherhood of men throughout the entire earth? *No, never.* Every interest appertaining to our nation, to humanity, to reason, to everything else, says, "However long this contest may be, we must at least never yield it up by granting the secession to the South." (Applause.)

Now come some enemies to the government, or rather, as they please to call themselves, enemies of the administration, and they are not small in number, who say, " we know it will never do to allow this nation to be broken in two, for that would be the end and ruination of our great republican institutions; but we should end this war by a *suitable and appropriate compromise* with them as soon as possible, and recover our disaffected brothers and friends back to the fellowship and amenities of our common family." Here, I say we have a large class of men, and a great many of them too are honest men, who think that about the only way to end this war, and that the true way is to offer terms of conciliation to those in rebellion, and such terms as they will accept, and consent to come back and unite their fate and history again with ours.

But there are some men in these ranks that are not honest men; and who do not move in this direction out of a pure love of the country, a pure desire for peace; and as I desired to speak historically and plainly on last Tuesday evening, permit me to speak plainly at this point to-night. I think that this cry for a compromise is a political cry, and instead of being (I make great exceptions) an honest declaration of the heart for peace and the adjustment of our country's difficulties, it is simply the plotting and scheming of politicians for the future welfare and position of their party. Let me illustrate this. About a year ago, I was in conversation with a prominent citizen of Trenton here, and he accosted me with this question, "What do you think of the war now-a-days?" Well, you remember about a year ago we were *blue* about the war. I was decidedly blue. "Well," said I, "I am a little down." "Well," said he, "what do you think will be the end of this thing?" "Well," I answered, "I think this will be the end. I think designing men will so far interfere with the movements of the government, and stay the progress of our arms, and hold back this war month after month, and year after year, until we get into another great Presidential campaign, and then you will most likely elect a Democratic President, and put a new party into power, and create a new administration, and then you will go forward with your old compeer of the South, and offer terms of concession, and they will accept them. You will then shake hands, take a drink, and it will be all over." "Now," said he, "you and I are pretty much alike, after all." "Yes." "Well," said he, "I am glad you have come to that ground. You and I hold the same opinion." "Yes," said, I, "that is my opinion, and that is where it will end. But there is as great a difference between you and me still, as between the north and south pole." "What is the difference?" said he; "I believe what you believe." "Yes," said I, "I believe it—sorrowfully and sadly believe it; but you hope for it, and work for it. That is the difference." And that is precisely the difference.

I come only to look in the face of this question, not for the sake of politicians, for they are keener than I am, but for the sake of honest

American citizens; and as I look into the face of this question of compromise, I am compelled as an honest patriot to say with regard to this, as with regard to a separation, " *No !*" this war cannot and ought not to end by compromises with the South. (Applause.) I looked into the South up as far as we could get the mail. I got Southern papers and read them over. I found in them the bitter spirit breathed out by these men. There was no indication there that the storm would ever end in compromise ; no terms to come back to the Union. They gloried in secession, and considered the act final and forever : they said no power of arms could bring them back into association again with the Yankee and with the Northern government. I look to this day as far as I can, and *I never heard of one single offer of compromise* or asking for terms on the part of the South ; but I find on the contrary only in the North, and that too in a class of men whose associations hitherto have been intimately connected with the South, throwing out this doctrine of compromise and adjustment to the South. The South never asked for it. In the midst of death and desolation, with poverty and want staring them in the face, no man yet—except those who have come into our lines and have never been traitors to the country—no one who has lifted his hand in this Rebellion, has asked any terms or pointed to any by which he could be brought back again into the Union.

Shall we end this war by any compromise with the South ? What I mean by compromise is making such concessions to them as will satisfy them, and will bring them back to their allegiance and submission to the government of the country. I have answered *no.* The first reason is, they have never asked for it ; and I can look upon it in no other light than as pusillanimous in the extreme, for a great government to go forward in this gigantic Rebellion, and call these men to come back by offering terms of compromise, and thus purchasing their friendship.

Let me draw your attention to a point in which lies a sophistry which is played on the minds of many men in these war times. There is a great difference between repentant *rebels coming forward to ask terms from the government against which they have rebelled, and that government coming forward and offering terms to rebels still in arms.* Where in history have you read of a government that came forward to rebels yet in arms, pressing every resource at their command into the service of treason ; where have you yet seen a government, unless that government was powerless or subdued, that came forward and sued for terms at the hands of rebels ? Shall we, this new born nation of Freedom, this great Republic, shall we teach this pusillanimous stooping of the government, to come and beg at the hands of traitors in arms ? *No, never,*

never! (Applause.) You may say it is philanthropy. No, it would be meanness to the utmost extreme. It would be philanthropy that would bring eternal infamy and disgrace upon the nation. Here is just the point where that grand message that we read awhile ago coming from a certain governor that called a certain class of people his friends, (laughter) in which he played off this great sophistry upon the amnesty proclamation of the President of the United States. I like that amnesty proclamation very much. I think it is just about the thing. It is just about as far as the President ought to have gone to maintain the dignity and honor of the government. He could have gone no farther. What was the point in the grand message that pleased some people in the month of December? That amnesty means nothing, it offers nothing to these men. It selects a party. It cries out to one-tenth of the people in the South, if you come back and lay down your arms we will receive you into the government again; you may organize your legislatures, elect your governors, and take your places in the Union with all your rights sacred, except one alone. I say that was a generous offer coming from a government to rebels in arms. Mr. Lincoln said, "I do not say that these are the only terms that shall be offered to men returning to their allegiance." He knew if the men would ground their arms, if they would cease their treason against the government, and come forward and say, "now we are ready to come back, what terms will you give us?" then would have been the time, and not till then, to make large and generous terms. Let Mr. Davis come, let the Masons, the Slidells and Cobbs, come and say, "We are done with the Rebellion, now what will the government offer as terms of concession," and you will find as big a heart as ever beat in one of the largest men that ever lived open to receive them on the most generous terms the government could offer. (Laughter and applause.) That is my first reason. They have not come forward to ask for compromise.

We cannot compromise because of the large multitude of men in the South that would be sacrificed by this very means. There are men in the South who have never sympathized with this Rebellion, and others little connected with the great evil of the nation. They have loved our history and love our nation until this day. They have spoken out boldly and fearlessly against this outrage of the nation. These are the men that would be sacrificed to the Union by a compromise. Said the Governor of New York in his note to the President, "it is selecting a party." To be sure it is selecting a party; but a party who stood true to the government. Why should he not have said, "as soon as you can rally one-tenth of the population we will acknowledge you as true and loyal citizens of the United States." Compromises would inflict calamities for years to come. There is a passage in the good old book which was recorded of a rebellion long ago, complaining of those who would heal too lightly the hurt of the people, and which applies to this Rebellion. I am not ready, for one, to enter into terms of compromise with the men that created this Rebellion. I want them punished severely.

One of the strange things of this war is the difficulty with which we realize the enormity of the crime committed by these men. We may love their souls, and if they would come forward and be honest citizens of the United States we would share our last loaf of bread with Jeff. Davis himself; but Jeff. Davis, arch traitor, and we, are enemies so long as he is arch traitor, (applause) or any other man in the South so long as he goes against the government of our country and against humanity. We talk to-day of these slaveholders—" Oh, they are our brothers." They are bad brothers then, and need whipping. We say, " they have been associated with us in the past." So they have, and we are bad teachers or we would have taught them better things. They have plotted for more than thirty years for this wrong, to let loose the dogs of war upon this peaceful land, scattering death and desolation over the plains of this country; put thousands of families into mourning; opened up hundreds of thousands of graves to their fellow men; shed seas of blood in accomplishing one of the most damnable schemes that ever was conceived by the mind of man; and yet these sickly philanthropists come forward and say, "don't hurt them." They ought to be hurt. They deserve to be hurt. Men who have awakened anguish and sorrow, and started tears, and spread desolation and havoc throughout this land, deserve the execration of men down to the end of time. (Applause.) I have said it is almost impossible for us (but I don't know why, it must be because of the generous principles of the government under which we live,) to realize the crime of treason. Treason! it is the blackest deed that can be committed in the sight of heaven. Treason! it is the forfeiture of every right that appertains to man. But what kind of treason is this? Treason of the deepest, darkest, and blackest die. Treason against the noblest government the world has had in all its history! Treason against the brightest hopes of humanity! Treason against the most plainly written indications of Divine Providence itself! Why He has not let the thunderbolt fall upon this people in the very act of so terrible a treason, I know not—that must lie in the counsels of the Almighty himself. No, I recall that. Most fearfully has the Judge of all the earth let His thunderbolts fall upon this guilty people. I pity their plains drenched in blood; I pity their soil upturned by the ploughshare of war; I pity their empty and desolate households, their poverty-stricken land. Ah, yes! they have drawn down upon themselves a terrible judgment from the hand of God.

I have another reason why I cannot go this compromise doctrine. It is this, *I am afraid of it.* I am afraid to try it. I don't want the South to come back as it was back for twenty-five or thirty years in the past. I know it is a dangerous thing to say that I am not in favor of the "*Union as it was ;*" and yet I am ready to say it. I hope that we shall never have again this Union as it was. (Applause.) The Union! I would give my life for it, and I would do anything in my power to restore to peace and union our sorely stricken country; but the Union such as we have had it for twenty years Heaven cannot smile upon. A Union such as we have had, would be but to rush forward again in the mad career of political strife, to end in a few years more in another contest more bloody and terrible than this. I want *no* Union with the groans of four millions of souls going up to the throne of God. (Applause.) I want no Union with representatives from one section standing upon the floor of Congress pistoled or caned to command votes, and stamping their foot upon the necks of Northern freemen. (Applause.) I want no Union in which I can travel South of Mason and Dixon's line only at the peril of my life. (Applause.) I want no Union where one section undertakes to claim the right to open up the United States mail bags, and examine all their contents, to see if anything is there incendiary or dangerous in its character. (Applause.) I want no Union, the foundation of one side of which rests on *hemp, and tar, and feathers.* (Laughter.) No, let us have such a Union as God intended it should be; as our fathers intended, where we shall have free speech, free press, and *free men* from Maine to the Gulf, and from the Atlantic to the Pacific. (Applause.) Now suppose you enter into a compromise with this party; suppose we say to the Southern States, "Come back, and we'll give you your price; we'll grant all you want, we perhaps made a mistake on the slavery question, and were perhaps in too great a hurry,"—and if they should come back, how long would it be until all these demands, all these intrigues upon liberty, all these disgraceful acts in the Congress of the United States, and this party scheming and political machinery, would again be at work in our land? I cannot consent to a compromise that only lays the foundation for future troubles, and for perpetual infamy and disgrace to rest upon the nation.

4

But I have yet another reason why I cannot go this compromise. There are four parties in this contest. Two of them we are exceedingly prone to forget and ignore. The government is upon one side, struggling in her integrity; and the Rebellion is on the other, gigantic and mighty in her spirit of revolution. Between the two lies a helpless race, numbering four millions of people—a third party. And above them all, the God and Father of all, whose eyes look down upon all his children. You *dare not* compromise with wrong when parties like these are in the field. God has let you move along in comparative quiet these eighty years in the past, until the mad tyrant lifted up the dagger to strike at the nation's heart; then God seized the dagger for Himself, and sent it back to the heart of the assassin. (Applause.) God has come upon the stage, and is working in this nation. Who has not heard the stepping of His feet? Who has not seen the moving of His Divine hand as He has steadily moved forward from the first outbreaking of this war until now, saying, "*You* began it, and *I* will end it; *let my bondsmen go.*" (Applause.) Now you will come forward in the face of events such as our war has been writing during the past two and a half years, and, in the face of God, cry for a pusillanimous peace by selling four millions of your fellow-men! The heavens would grow dark above us, and infamy eternal from all the nations of the earth would settle upon us. *You*, the advocates of liberty! *You*, the friends of human rights! *You*, the leading nation of the globe! *You* that are the hope of the future ages of the earth! *You* pusillanimously stoop to buy peace from men in rebellion by selling back to bondage four millions of your helpless fellow-men! *No! no!* God and humanity forever forbid that at such a price we shall buy peace in our land. (Applause.) Have you any other compromise to offer? Buy peace with what? With the negro? What else have you to say to Davis, then? "Get down off your throne and we'll give you Sambo." What have you to say to men in arms? Down with your arms and we'll send the *nigger* back. *The negro is not yours to give,* and God will not allow him to be sent back, except with broken shackles. Woe to this nation, or that party, that *dares* buy back again these rebels at the price of human blood. (Applause.)

"You cannot allow them to separate? *No.* Cannot compromise with them? *No,* not on that question. What then? There is one way left yet. What is it? *Whip it out of them.* (Long-continued and loud applause.) That is about the true doctrine. (Applause.) Go right forward. Whip them into submission. You seem to understand the thing exactly. (Laughter.) I wonder why I was invited to lecture about "How to get out," when you all know how to get out? (Applause.) You see the point as well as I do. (Laughter.) The instincts of common honest men and women point the road to independence, to liberty; and that road is by gathering together the strong forces of the government and rolling them upon this Rebellion, and crushing it beneath the power of the nation.

Now I am in favor of two things some people are not in favor of—*coercion* and *subjugation*. If you would ask me again to put into other words what I have said—what is the true method of getting out of this war?—I would say coercion and subjugation. We used to be terribly frightened over these two words; yet, when we come to look at them, they are a mere bug-bear after all. Coercion! What does that mean? My wife coerces me every day (laughter), and I am exceedingly fond of the coercion. My little children coerce me every day. I like to be coerced. You see the word is not frightful. It is altogether in its application it has been made to appear so. In some relations it is delightful; in others it is not so good. In this war it is simply making those men do their duty; making them behave themselves; making them stop the Rebellion and lay down their arms; making them become citizens of the United States, and *whipping them until they do*. (Applause.) I have been coerced now nearly forty years by this government, and I never felt it hard; it sets easy. Yet the government coerces you and me every day. We don't dare to steal. Why? Because the government coerces us. We don't dare to commit murder. Why? Because the government coerces us. We don't dare to be anything else than honest, peaceful citizens of the state and of the United States. Why? It is the terrible government that is coercing us. We want Jeff. Davis coerced as we are, so that he shall not steal, and shall not commit murder, and shall not rise up in arms against the government; that he shall be the honest, straightforward citizen of that United States government that we are. (Applause.) What else can you mean by subjugation? Peace needs no buying. You don't buy war. What do you mean by subjugation? We mean South Carolina shall behave herself like New Jersey, and shall come back again under the stars and stripes (applause), and shall send her representatives to Washington instead of Richmond, and shall move forward in honest obedience to the government of the United States, under which she was made all that she is. We have had a terrible outcry against coercing and subjugating states. Mr. Lincoln's idea of it is correct—to whip them until one-tenth are ready to come back, then receive them, and let that be a state of honest, true, and loyal men. (Applause.)

Now when we talk about war as a means of bringing the war to an end, some say "you have become bloodthirsty; you have become imbued with the spirit of war." I answer *No*, I can only look upon it as the highest Christianity, and I can only see in it the purest charity, to go vigorously and earnestly at work, and bring it to an end as speedily as possible. Bring all the forces of this great government to bear on this Rebellion, and before 1864 closes you will have the Rebellion closed, and this waste of life and treasure put an end to. It is this miserable delaying, this holding back, this lying in swamps where soldiers die by thousands, this wasting of life and treasure, that is most cruel and impolitic. It is true charity to bring forth the nation's strength and press the war with vigor and energy. Do you want the war ended before 1864 shall end? Then work for the government. Rush to the standard of the nation. Come one, come all, and march down to the South in one grand solid phalanx. Present bristling fronts of bayonets to the rebels in arms; one more vigorous and stirring effort, and ere this year passes away you will see the end of the war, and that you are safely out. Let us consent for a little while to forget party, to forget politics, to forget the offices of the future, and stand once together to show the strength of our government, and see what results can be accomplished by this steady, straightforward, and simple course.

I think we have done remarkably well in this war. It has not been a long war; we have not yet been engaged three years in it. It has been a gigantic struggle; history will furnish no greater one in all its records of the past; and yet more than half of this rebel territory is under the guardianship of the glorious old banner of the stars and stripes. (Applause.) More than five and a half millions of the population of the rebel states are again under the shelter of the government. Tennessee is nearly all back. Kentucky has been taught her serious and sorrowful lessons, and is quiet, and peaceful, and loyal. She has had enough of war and bloodshed. *My* Maryland will not be disturbed in the future. Arkansas is ready to come in. Texas is moving, and a large portion of Louisiana is ours. North Carolina is trembling like a needle to the old pole that she used to love. While the war is well nigh over, we have done the hardest part of the work. Who does not see plainly that to conquer the first half of the Rebellion—and the first half of its wicked population—to bring them again over from this Rebellion under the influence and power of the government, is not to have accomplished vastly more than half the great result. I think the administration has done well. I like good old honest Abraham (applause), who started out into the world exceedingly poor. The Cobbs and the Floyds left him almost a beggar when he commenced house-keeping—our ships were all away, the treasury was emptied, and rebellion was staring him in the face; and yet how calm the old man has been with it all! I have admired that very spirit of honest joking that sits so calmly on the face of this man, who has the weight of a nation upon him, as if he could see it all from the beginning to the end. Trusting in the God of battles, he can be even cheerful while he guides the great ship through the shoals and breakers. (Applause.) I say he has done well in the course of these three years past : and one thing allow me to say at the close, I think the best method of getting out of the war is to give him another turn for the presidency. (Applause.) He has his hand in it, is quite well acquainted with it, and I would not like to risk new hands. Give Abraham a chance to finish, and we'll enshrine his name alongside the first and best of all names,—" *Abraham, the good President*," who safely led us out from the terrible realities of war. For, with such a cause to inspire our efforts, and with the smile of heaven and the approval of the common instincts of humanity all over the world, we cannot fail. We will come out of it rightly, as the morning sun breaks out of the dews that cloud his rising. Come out of it ? Yes; better than when we went into it—a strong, a free, and brave people, and honored throughout the world as having stood true to our government, true to our God, and true to our common humanity. (Long and enthusiastic applause.)